MW01015482

A Taste
of Living
in Mexico

A collection of stories and
suggestions for
would-be gringos

by Leo Buijs

Stories and suggestions for would-be gringos

First edition 2016

National Library of Canada Cataloging in Publication

Buijs, Leo,
      Living/ Retiring in Mexico/ Mexico travel/ Leo Buijs

Includes index.
ISBN 978-0973552768

1. Living or Retiring in Mexico 2. Mexico Travel information 3. guidebook to living or retiring in Mexico 4. Baja California – Mexico – I Title

This book is published by Seaview Investments Ltd., 219 Spindrift Rd, Courtenay B.C. V9N 9S9 Canada

E-mail: leobuijs@yahoo.ca

Cover design and layout: Desgraph.Ltd

.... Could it be that Americans are a restless people, a mobile people, never satisfied with where they are as a matter of selection?

From travels with Charley, by John Steinbeck

Other books by

Leo Buijs

50 Best Dog Walks Around Victoria
2003

Best Dog Walks on Vancouver Island
2008

Beers of British Columbia
2010

Children around the World
2015 edition

Children around the World
large coffee-table edition
2016

Map of Mexico

Table of Contents

Stories and suggestions for would-be gringos

Introduction

Millions of people vacation every year in Mexico. How many of them, while there, being lazy on a beach or next to a pool with a tasty margarita or cool beer in hand, are having visions of that life on a permanent basis? A second home, away from home or a complete change of lifestyle and settling permanently somewhere in Mexico.

Some people would trade their hurried lifestyle in a wink if they could. Others would be a bit more careful and check out what options there are and how they can accomplish that dream.

This book is for both: fast movers and the more 'wait and see' types. Both of you will find a lot of useful substance in this book despite keeping the selection of stories light and tasty. The more serious information on how and what it all entails to become an expat in Mexico can be found in the follow-up on this book called 'Living or Retiring in Mexico'. Both books contain a wealth of information and actual experiences I learned during 15 years of traveling, living and retiring in Mexico with my wife and dog.

As a habit, I always have been taking travel notes, often at nocturnal hours, wherever we went. We did it all: frequent traveling throughout this beautiful and cultural diverse country, rented long-term accommodations in different States and eventually bought and built a house with ocean view and a five-minute walk to an unspoiled beach. Those things are possible in Mexico and you don't have to be very rich to accomplish that. But it has been a long and steady up-hill learning curve for us and you can take advantage of it by harvesting the results. We have experienced first-hand the ups and downs about living and owning real-estate in Mexico and as they say; "I can write a book about it."

And so I did.

This book however, is very different from all the books available on this subject. During one of our extended stays in 2001, I picked up a writing job as a freelance journalist for a bi-weekly English language newspaper in Mexico.

As it happened, my earliest experience was a local event I wrote about, submitted to the local English language newspaper and had it published instantly. Twelve years later I was still writing for that same paper with a deadline every other week, which was a great thing for an early retired guy like me. To have a dead-line every other week surely kept me on my toes and out of trouble. For over a decade I have been writing on subjects like fiestas, cultural events, Mexican bureaucracy, and what to do and not to do in Mexico. Some of the best articles of that time are used or updated and therefore you will get a real taste of living in Mexico in the following chapters.

-0-0-0-0-

What attracts foreigners to live in Mexico?

There are a million answers to this simple question. Perhaps John Steinbeck touch a cord when he wrote in Travels *with Charley*, "Could it be that Americans and Canadians are a restless people, a mobile people, never satisfied with where they are as a matter of selection?"

When I asked people why, the majority fell into three categories; the weather, to be out of the rat-race and the different culture.

Many books have been written about Americans retiring to Mexico to live out their Golden Years. However, in the last five years I have seen an increasing number of younger people moving to Mexico, not necessarily to retire but to further their career alongside a different life style. Working long-distance with the help of internet and having the time of their life at the same time. Some are finding existing local needs and start their own businesses to tap into that need. These folks are called the new Expats.

Many people have the false impression that you find a simpler life-style in Mexico. And that is true to a certain extent and the weather has a lot to do with this. But everyday life can turn out to be a nuisance at times.

Think about water: if you are lucky it runs from your tap every morning, is most of the time not potable, at times lacking pressure or at odd times not even available. So you need to be flexible and sparse with water. Better still is to have a certain capacity of reserve water for your shower or laundry. For drinking and washing your vegetables and berries, you bring in the large heavy 19 liter blue bottles. Living off grid poses other problems such as battery maintenance and cleaning of your sun panels on regular intervals. Safety and a language barrier present other issues that come to mind, but they offer also a challenge. Learning a new language can be exciting and fulfilling by itself.

Perhaps other things make up for the inconvenience, like living closer to nature, maybe within view of an unspoiled beach. As land is relatively cheap, you might have a larger property than you would have had north of the border. With that you might get the problem of hiring a gardener. Of course, all those things can be managed by a property management company, but that comes usually with a North American price tag.

Choosing to live in a town or a larger, perhaps historical city, water and electricity are less of a problem and or completely out of your control.

Still, a lot of us would take some inconveniences to get out of the rat-race, leaving that stressful life behind and acquire a new lifestyle. To live in a different, warm and sunny country where you can be anybody you would like to be without pretense. This, among other things, has a perpetual pull to *'la Viva Loca'* in Mexico. Not everybody is cut out for this and that's why not everyone's dream comes through. It takes a certain personality to make that big step. Many of our friends and acquaintances in Mexico are 'different' to say the least. Individualistic characters are the most common denominator.

Creative individuals, often with artistic aspirations live next to renegades, non-conformists, freaks and oddballs or occasionally, plain nuts. But the beauty of it is that in this climate and culture one gets away with most of his or her idiosyncrasies.

There is a saying by boaters about ownership. It says: his best days were the day he got his boat and the other day was when he sold it. Well, this could also be said about owning a house in Mexico, but I have to admit that the time in between has been very exciting and educational and that is what this book is all about.

This book is a compilation of Mexican adventures, experiences, food and fiestas, put together and easy to read as each part contains smaller chapters revealing life in Mexico.

My story is based upon observations and firsthand experiences during some decades traveling to and living half of that time in Mexico. I make no pretense to thoroughness, but have tried. It is the same for objectivity, which was not easy.

All information including tips on location and geographical differences, climate, prices, tax and government related info such as customs immigration etcetera are believed accurate at the time of writing. As things can change rather quickly in Mexico, I cannot be held liable for changes, omissions or mistakes. Thank you for getting this book, and enjoy the ride!

-0-0-0-0-

If not for this book, where to start?

To get a real taste of Mexico, my advice is to take some trips to different parts of Mexico as the country is quite large and very different from one part to the other. Perhaps you have done that already and found out that not everyone likes to spend all their time on the beach or besides a pool. Central Mexico with it's mountains and historic towns have a totally different climate compared to the coastal areas and a different culture, and an even warmer climate can be found further south.

My wife and I have been traveling to Mexico many times for shorter trips, and then one year, we were in a position to explore this sunny and colorful country for months at the time. That was important for us to get a feel for it, to experience different areas and make a list of what our priorities were.

It turned out that for us, our stay should be drive-able. That does limit you if you don't want to spend half your time getting there and back. But the plus was to have a car and be able to bring lots of stuff including our inseparable house-pet: the dog. Not that you cannot fly with your dog, but it is limited. For instance, when temperatures heat up in April or May, airlines don't take dogs any more. Over the X-mas holidays, our carrier from Canada does not allow dogs in cargo. O.K., if you have a small *chihuahua*, you might put the little one under the seat, but larger size dogs have more restrictions.

So, connectivity either by road or plane can be an important factor for choosing your Mexican stay. I have been going to Mexico since 1984. First on the east side, the State of Yucatan with all its historic Mayan ruins, lovely beaches and superb diving spots around the island of Cozumel. I have been back there a few more times and it took until the late nineties that I finally decided to check out the Pacific side and Central Mexico with it's beautiful colonial cities.

On the Pacific side, we drove the entire Baja California peninsula, north and south, more then ten times. However, the first time we flew as part of a booked all-inclusive hotel package in San Jose del Cabo and extended our stay for a week or two to explore the rest of the southern peninsula. We rented a car and drove counter clockwise to check out the famous reef at Cabo Pulmo in the Sea of Cortez. We went on to the humble, at that time, little capital of the State, La Paz. It was very small and sleepy still, at that time, except for weekends on the Malecón After checking the beaches north from there, we went south-west to the sleepy town of Todos Santos.

Finding a hotel for a few nights was not easy. The now famous Hotel California was in disrepair, closed-up and for sale. We inquired about the price and what the options were, but never got an appointment to see the place inside. The few accommodations there were, were either cockroach infested, very cheap places or high-end luxury rooms in small historic haciendas.
There was virtually nothing in between, making the future of Hotel California a plausible success. We surely fell in love with the town. One morning at the beach, we had seen already several whales passing by, but then suddenly we saw a presumably, mother whale with a small calf playing, frolicking, not further out than perhaps 100 yards from the beach. Mommy showing the baby how to jump and roll in the waves. It was a breathtaking experience! Watching this from an unspoiled, virgin beach made this so much better and different from the tourist-trodden beaches of so many Mexican destinations. This was unbelievable! Baja California has miles of unspoiled beaches with whales passing by, up close from December to March.
All good things end to quickly, so we went on reluctantly to the spoiled tourist town of Cabo San Lucas to finish our circle and went home the next day. It took us a few years to come back but

not until after we checked out the Mexican mainland: Mexico City, Quaretaro, Guanajuato and San Miguel. Beautiful cities each in their own way. Historic pearls in a large quilt of places high in the mountains with colder temperatures in winter and no beaches. That made us decide to go back to Baja California in 2001. This was the first time we drove the entire length of the peninsula from the Tijuana border to San Jose at the Sea of Cortez. We had rented an apartment for a month in San Jose del Cabo and brought our bicycles to explore the area other than just by car. Our home-stay was close to the golf course and municipal tennis courts, so we played most mornings right at seven o'clock because later in the day it was quite hot that November.

A year later we rented a *casita* in Loreto, halfway down the Baja right on the Sea of Cortez. This was a spectacular setting, as every morning we had the sun come up out of the sea and burn through the thin curtains from where we saw the calm morning waters of the

Sea of Cortez with some islands speckled in the distance. By 10.30 it would become a different matter. The winds would pick up and transform the so quiet Sea of Cortez into a white capped fury by lunch time. The town has a nice older centre and historic mission. We explored the mountains and the shores far south and north from there. Our trip to the mission of San Javier, built in 1697, still standing and very isolated in the mountains at that time, was quite the adventure. Particularly the road up to it, as we had to cross river beds and steep mountain roads more like goat paths and only doable with a 4x4. Now that road is all black topped as far as I know. One has to go further into the mountains to find adventure.

After a month and a half we moved down to Todos Santos where we had booked a *casita* on the huge palm-covered grounds of artist Nanette Hayles. This was close to the centre of town and was the first year the Todos Santos Film Fest was organized. Everything was very informal, small scaled and personal. Also it was cold and rainy and the Theatre de Leon was a massive draft hole with concrete seats that numbed your butt in no time. Smart people brought pillows and blankets to make it through the often lengthy Mexican dramatic movies.

This trip in 2004 ultimately resulted in us buying a house in Mexico.

-0-0-0-0-

How friendly are Mexicans?

The other day I came across this blog from Chuck Poulsen that describes exactly the way Mexican are. I have had many instances of the same friendly behavior by Mexican strangers.

"There is a very large and upscale mall in Guadalajara called the Galerias. One of the anchors is Liverpool, a Mexican retailer that the shopping crowd equates to Saks Fifth Avenue. The other anchor is Sears, which in Mexico sells much higher quality (and priced) merchandise than Sears in Canada or the U.S., strangely enough.

The only thing that had me in an upscale mall was a search for a jacket and a couple of ball caps. Mexicans don't wear caps like up north; they're hard to find. I saw a teenager in a store wearing a cap, backwards, of course, and asked him where he got it. His mother was with the kid and told him to walk with me to the store and show

me where the caps were at.

All of this fuzzy, feel good news from an unexpected source, namely me, is because Mexicans get a bum rap from Canadians and Americans.

I've been to Mexico many times, and lived here for a couple of years awhile back.

Mexicans who live outside the tourist destinations are generally friendly, almost always helpful people with a very good sense of humor.

Of course, there are exceptions, but I dare say they are friendlier than your average Canadian or American."

To get in the mood

Imagine yourself on a patio with a margarita or Corona (fine, but not the best Mexican beer) and a plate full of quesadillas, Tabasco and guacamole on the side, a colorful tablecloth, the blue and white plastic table and chairs (provided by Corona) and an umbrella of course as it is sunny and warm. All Mexican icons in their own right and unmistakably part of the ex-pat's life in Mexico.

But there is so much more that makes Mexico, Mexico. Therefor I like to describe some typical Mexican styles that make homes and decorative items so special and appealing to us foreigners.

First the multi-hued, may I say wild color combinations are something that stands out almost everywhere in Mexico. From house colours to traditional clothing and interior decor items. Graceful arched verandas are combined with warm ochre coloured walls and checker-board tile floors.

Modern homes now also experiment with sort of the opposite; a Minimalist style, simple and earthy colours opposed to the wild colour schemes.

Classy homes often make use of a Boveda, meaning- vaulted, rounded ceiling.

For wall decoration one can find very interesting stenciled or painted wall bands.

Interesting textiles are often naturally dyed woolen blankets and sarapas that are handwoven and come in vibrant colours that differ from state to state. Some places however, seldom dye wool and leave shawls or bedspreads in their natural colour. A texture of white on white brocade makes for subtle table linen.

Strangler-root palm or strangled beams are used decoratively indoors and out and are not cheap as they have to come from central Mexico. Another wood, used mostly indoors as a ceiling beam, are hand-hewn bacote.

They are hand shaped hardwood beams that give lots of character to a house. An item that will give a nice touch to the interior are gauze-white curtains, while for the bedrooms sheer white mosquito netting might come in handy and will look very romantic.

A popular indoor outdoor furniture is called Equipal. This has a rather rough wooden frame with leather seating and backs. The inside can also be upholstered with the colourful fabrics that look so typical Mexican.

The extreme colorful and craftily painted furniture comes from a town in the State of Michoacan. The large black pots are made in Chihuahua.

Ceramic animals come from Oaxaca and they also make the beautiful jars, and urns are called *Tala Vera*. Most tiles come from the town of Dolores Hidalgo, central Mexico. Cheaper tiles are called *Pueblo* tiles which are brown and earthy in tone. Tin mirrors and lamps are mostly made in San Miguel.

Beautifully decorated ceramic sinks are very popular and hammered copper sinks are also prime choice for the bathroom.

The paper banners (they look a bit Nepalese) that you see hanging across streets or are used for decoration during parties or fiestas are called *Papel Picado*. Mexicans use multitudes of candles and you can find them in all shapes and sizes. Thinking of parties? They are often illuminated with *Luminarios*, wax-lights in brown paper bags that we also see used north of the border nowadays.

-0-0-0-0-

Todos Santos Early Days

During our second week stay we saw whales every day. Particularly off the beach by Todos Santos, where we had the best show of breaching Gray whales. A mother and calf were swimming side by side as if giving swimming lessons. Then they were jumping and tail smashing, excitement galore. We loved the little town of Todos Santos, so green and authentic with a lot of tasteful galleries and a few historic buildings. The saying about Todos Santos is that it's the only place in Mexico where there are more art galleries than taco stands. Now don't get me wrong, but if you are looking for a tasty bite on the street, there are plenty of taco stands. Art galleries however, are numerous and of great quality.

We stayed a few extra days and had a good cappuccino with breakfast, local beers with lunch and Baja wine with dinner. That wine brought back memories from a trip to Kenya where we also paid a fortune for not such very good local wine. The alternative, import was out of reach! So what do you drink? (This has changed marvelously, the quality of the wine that is. However, the price is still high or equivalent to the price of wine north of the border.)

It was easy to fall in love with Southern Baja and Todos Santos in specific because of the weather and the endless options for water-sports. Surfing and beach combing nearby while snorkeling, diving, kayaking and sailing are possible almost everywhere else. Whale watching, same thing, absolutely tops! The moderate temperature and the fact that it has over 300 days of sunshine per year are hard to beat.

-0-0-0-0-

Practice makes Perfect.
(Friends of us that stayed at an all inclusive)

After a lapse of several years, Frank and Charlene, a semi-retired stock broker and his trophy wife stepped off the plane in San Jose. It was a gorgeous afternoon, maybe a bit on the warm side for a couple that just escaped the long dark winter north of the 49th parallel. Not that they lived in igloos up there as most Americans believe, but a change for warmer climes can be nice once in a while. They were looking forward to make peaceful use of their time-share they were talked into when they were in Cabo and had a few drinks too many a few years ago.

Frank is still puzzled about that purchase. He does not even like hot climates because he cannot show off his favorite tie and jacket and refuses to wear shorts. The sun will do more damage then good to his pale skin and balding head he thinks, making him a good candidate for a large sombrero. But Frank would rather spend his money on brand-name designer clothes and shoes. His lovely wife on the other hand, adores the sun and she could not wait to get her tight little butt on a lounge-chair next to a pristine pool.

Once through customs, Frank found out that there isn't much choice in taxis as they have set rates and are all controlled by the same company. A giant Mexican chauffeur ushered them to a big SUV which they needed for their oversize luggage. In the car, Charlene pushed the windows down and let the wind ruffle her long blond hair during the speedy ride along the toll road to the hotel strip.

Since their time-share purchase they have used their week at many other places and when they arrived at the hotel, they didn't recognize the place.

A huge, iridescent green banner screamed 'Welcome to sales team USA.' The once pastoral setting was now cluttered with many more hotels all around. They also noticed that the hotel was not really kept up too well despite their yearly increasing maintenance fees and to make things worse, the place was booked that week for a national Gatorade sales convention. A 4-story high blow-up juice bottle and a massive alligator were swaying in the wind while loud blaring music was echoing through the corridors when they checked in.

Frank however, likes quiet times, reading, and playing classical music for which he had brought a few instruments which explains the bulky luggage. At home, he practices his music almost obsessively, one hour, early, every morning before he goes to his brokerage office in town. When they booked their stay, he had specifically requested a corner room so only neighbors on one side would have to keep up with his practice. Frank obviously didn't remember that the walls were more like cardboard, so that did not work out too well.

After one morning of ardent trying to master some complicated passages in Paganini's cello concerto, the front desk called about the neighbors in room 213. They had complained that someone might have a cat in the room which makes horrible sounds at an unacceptable time in the morning. The next day Frank practiced later in the morning so the busy sounds of cleaning crew, room-service, traffic and overhead air-planes would cover his attempts to attack Paganini again. This was not only nicer for the neighbors in 213 but suited his wife much better also, as by that time, the pool would be open and she could install herself close to the bar instead of suffering the early morning practice in the room with supper-sized earplugs in her cute little ears.

On one of his walks a few days later, Frank explored the beach and found a beautiful spot behind a rock formation, out of the way from the hotel rooms and he decided to play there one of his other instruments, the flute, next morning at sunrise.

Armed with a flashlight and one of his favorite silver flutes, Frank has a whole collection of them, a music stand, sheet music of some popular classics and a ball-cap as it was still a bit chilly, Frank sneaked out of the room and went to the beach. Once set up behind the rocks, he got so inspired that he played piece after piece without interruptions or mistakes. After the sun came up higher in the sky, he started to perspire and put his ball-cap upside down on the ground in front of him. By now, several joggers were running along the beach and one of them stopped to listen for a while. Frank was totally not used to perform for strangers, he got nervous and missed a note or two. The jogger felt sorry for him and dropped a twenty peso bill in the hat of a by now flabbergasted stockbroker. Then, as the jogger went on his way again, the jogger said "Keep on playing senor, practice makes perfect."

"OK" said Frank, "and you keep running, keeps you in shape!"

-0-0-0-0-

The Fun Stuff

Fiestas in Mexico

It is said that fiestas claim 317 days a year in the historic town of San Miguel de Allende. National holidays- and religious are only a small part of the mix. Every town has their own celebrations, often around their patron's day. Some are at the same time and others are at different times at different locations throughout Mexico. This means that at any given time, there is a fiesta going on somewhere in Mexico. Someone who checked this out, claims that there are only nine days left, that go without a fiesta somewhere in all of Mexico.

In the next couple of pages, you find a small selection of some fiestas. One National, followed by a non-National, regional fiesta.

Independence Day, Viva Mexico

For good reason, September in Mexico is called *Mes de la Fiestas Patrias,* month of national festivities and so after a long boring summer the fiesta scene is finally heating up. And so is everything else this time of year, the weather hot and humid, locals excited about their fiestas and gringos planning their return

.

About a week prior to *Dia de la Indepencia* you may see many street vendors setting up shop at the busy corners all over town in preparation for the fiesta on September 16. This is considered the most important Mexican national holiday, equivalent to the 4th of July in the USA. And they are patriotic all right, the Mexicans, no less than gringos. Street vendors will be peddling besides the usual refreshments and snacks, all sorts of patriotic wares.

This is a good time to buy national flags that are available in all sizes, streamers and even candies that are now in the important three national colors of red, white and green. Remember this; the colors all symbolize something different and represent important parts in the celebrations. The green, on the left side of the flag symbolizes hope and independence. The white section in the middle symbolizes religion and purity and red on the right, symbolizes union and the blood of the fallen national heroes.

On September 16, 1810, the rebellion started on mainland Mexico which eventually led to Mexico's independence from the 'mother-land' Spain. Be aware that this is a statutory holiday all over Mexico with banks and government offices closed. Comparing the US Independence Day with Mexico's, you will notice that Mexicans are way more emotional than gringos. This huge fiesta is a two-day affair as the party always starts the evening before. That evening, it will be busy on the streets and you can feel the excitement building particularly in the centers of town, and around city hall. The climax is exact at 11 pm, when the Mayor will kick-start the party with the independence yell called *El Grito*, the start-sign for a patriotic party that can last all night long. Everyone will copy and will yell 'Viva Mexico' three times as loud as they can.

The most dramatic and impressive celebrations are held in Mexico City and in Dolores Hidalgo, the town where the reading of the Declaration of Independence originally took place. The leader of the independence movement was Father Hidalgo, the spiritual leader of Dolores. When he learned on September 15, 1810, that a conspiracy against the ruling Spanish had been discovered by the authorities, he had no choice but to start the rebellion. It was Hidalgo who rang the church bell and shouted the cry for independence. That very same bell is now on the balcony of the National Palace in Mexico City where the president commemorates this historic event every year. At 11 pm sharp Enrique Peña Nieto, the current President of the republic will ring this historic bell and will shout over the large *Zocalo* the names of the heroes of the revolution and ending with *"Viva Mexico" "Viva la independencia."* The crowd, waiting in anticipation, echoes back as loud as they can *"Viva Mexico"* while the air fills with confetti, streamers and noise you cannot imagine. From all directions, paper *Castillos* explode in showers of red, white, and green, the national colors of course. This tradition is observed all over Mexico, with so much gusto throughout the night, that no one can escape this party.

Closer to home, patriotic Mexicans decorate their house for this occasion with flags in windows and put them on cars just as when their national soccer team was playing for the world-cup. No fiesta goes without traditional food. On the evening of September 15, Mexicans prepare a special corn-meal, *pozole* and *buñuelos*, and enjoy dinner together with the family before they go to the central square or municipal hall. In Baja's State capital of La Paz, colorful festivities are held in the center of town while everywhere else, the big event will be the parade on the morning of *Dia de la Independencia*. School kids, politicians and many people from different organizations will proudly parade through the streets.

Most larger towns organize fairs and rodeos that are great fun for all walks of life and can be a great opportunity for gringos to experience the Mexican spirit.

Food of course, is a major part of these festivities. Road stands will offer the traditional *antojitos*, strictly translated as 'little whims,' a tasty variety of small appetizers. A huge selection of Mexican candies can be found that could be washed down with *ponche*. This *ponche*, or punch, is made of fruits that are now in season: particularly guayabas, sugarcane, mango and apples. It has a delicious aroma.

Villista Cavalcade Fiesta

There is a time of year that National or religious fiestas are as scarce as there are bottles of beer left in my fridge after a long weekend. That is when they make up some secular fiestas, just to have fun or to pump money into the local economy.

A truly Mexican fiesta in mid-summer is *Villista Cavalcade,* a week long fiesta around mid-July. It's held in Chihuahua, capital of the Mexican state by the same name, to commemorate the assassination of that revolutionary rascal *Pancho Villa.*

Who has not heard about *Francisco "Pancho" Villa*, the leading figure in the 1910 Mexican Revolution? "Of all Mexican Revolution leaders, no one was as controversial as *Francisco Villa*" according to *Jorge Carrera*, president of the Chihuahuan Culture Institute. *"No one has remained as strongly in people's memory as he has."* Perhaps his importance is fading now that "the short one, *El Chapo'* was captured in early 2016. But that is another story. This *Villista Cavalcade* fiesta attracts many performances of classical and folk music and groups of minstrels strolling through the historic center of Chihuahua. However, the absolute highlight of the fiesta is the *cavalcade* itself, a parade on horseback from the city of Chihuahua to Hidalgo del Parral, some 136 miles away, where *Pancho's* assassination took place.

Since its first occurrence, this rambunctious cavalcade has grown progressively larger. Over 1,000 horseback riders are expected to participate and about 400 motorcyclists are joining the fun in recent years. Can you imagine the dust? A hankie for your face might come in handy and don't forget a few six-packs to quench the thirst.

Getting there can be an adventure by itself. Not so much if you simply take a plane, but if you like me, take the ferry north from La Paz across the Sea of Cortez and go over land, it will be. Prepare for a choppy boat ride to Topolobampo, then a fast taxi into Los Mochis where you buy a ticket for that famous '*Chepe*' train ride, right through the massive Copper Canyon district to Chihuahua. This is an absolutely spectacular trip and worth every peso.

Think about this for a moment: going to celebrate an assassination. Isn't that what we love about Mexico? No scruples with mortality. Remember 'Day of the Death' in November? Anyway, *Pancho's* assassination actually happened on July 20, 1923 and only in Mexico, this calls for a boisterous party. Perhaps it is just smart thinking on the part of the tourist office in Chihuahua where they only two decades ago came up with this fiesta to honor *Francisco Villa*. His death is reconstructed every year on the exact spot where it happened.

Pancho Villa

Re-enactments are popular in Mexico and as if there are not enough casualties in the northern States in real life, a few dressed-up characters as *Pancho* and his cronies get a number of rubber bullets fired into them when they appear in their 1919 Dodge sedan from around a corner. Pancho's body took the brunt of the assault and died almost instantly while his hands were reaching for his gun. His skull was robbed from his grave and is still missing but the original Dodge is in the local museum where you can put your fingers in all the bullet holes from that day in 1923.

If you ever make it to Chihuahua, *Pancho's* former classy residence is turned into that museum where the Dodge is displayed in the courtyard. It's really worth a visit and why not combine it with a clamorous party at the same time?

-0-0-0-0-

Snorkeling and diving

Mexico has many good diving and snorkeling places. One of the best is off the east-side of the southern Baja Peninsula at Cabo Pulmo. The reef just about 100 yards off the shore of Cabo Pulmo, is a huge preserved area in the Sea of Cortez. It is world-famous for its splendor and large variety in fish and coral. On the Mexican Gulf side, the Island of Cozumel was an absolute high-light when I dove there. Guess, divers usually know their favorite destinations, so I will leave it at that.

One popular destination out of Cabo is Santa Maria's cove. This beautiful crested cove has reefs at both ends where the waves break and the snorkeling is at it's best. The temperature can be a bit on the cool side but the variety of fish and coral is not bad. There isn't much shade here so we rented an umbrella for a few hours. Then the crowds came in and with them the local merchants.

"Special price for you."

"Wanne look at my junk?"

"T-shirts or hats?"

A short while later they came with eatables, fruit, drinks you name it, and we almost found a need for something, "What about two Corona's" I asked.

"No Signor, no beer on beach."

What nonsense that is! Next time we know now what to bring, and a sign to put up saying "we don't buy anything, Thanks for not disturbing". You must give them credit for ingenuity and persistence however. The way they stack all their merchandise from the hips up or hang it all on sticks carried over their shoulders. Always trying and always coming back half an hour later just in case you have changed your mind.

Whale Watching near Guerrero Negro

There are several good places for whale watching in Mexico. Most are on the Pacific coast of Baja California. On our way south we stopped halfway down the Baja, right at the border of North and Southern Baja where Pacific time zone changes into Mountain time.

At 8 am, we left in a small bus with 12 other gringos of which two were a typically gay couple, both hairdressers living in Tijuana but working in San Diego. Imagine the daily commuting over that busy border crossing! They were funny and had the right attitude to deal with that.

The bus took us all the way through town towards the salt-pans and shipping area where the salt is collected and the docks are. The salt storage is in huge piles, mountains, that look as white as alpine ski hills, complete with avalanche tracks from salt that has slid down the slopes.

Just past the salt-barges, two *pangas* were ready to take us out on "Scammon's Lagoon." A twenty-five-minute ride at full-speed got us to the first group of Gray whales. They are very common here in January and February and can amount to about 2000 at a given time in the lagoon. There supposed to be four baby whales in the bay, but we didn't see any that day. Instead, we saw several groups of very active, sexually active, whales. Usually five to seven whales of which one or two were clearly female, smaller, and were humped several times by the large bulls. The satisfaction must have reached sensational proportions to the result that some whales breached free from the water out of exultation. Imagine, 35 tons of mass jumping out of the ocean! Thanks god, we were at a respectable distance.

On the way back, we finished prepackaged lunches that were provided and watched immense large salt-barges moving by. Empty ones being pushed back fast, for miles to the loading dock and full ones pulled slowly out into deeper ocean waters to be transferred over to deep-sea cargo ships. By noon, we were back at our motel, changed into shorts and walked our dog.

-0-0-0-0-

Food and Drinks

Mexican Beer

It is hard to imagine any fiesta in Mexico without *cerveza*. Beer has become the most popular drink to celebrate anything in Mexico. Even on non-fiesta days, beer consumption has reached huge proportions per capita. Several factors have played a role in beer's popularity. History for one and low taxation in the 1900's to keep the cost down so peasants would switch from the rather damaging habits of drinking *Pulque* (pronounced pool-kay) to *cerveza*. Then came a wide availability of beers and last but not least, an insatiable thirst in a hot and dusty country that has made beer the most popular drink in Mexico.

Before the existence of beer, the Aztecs and Mayas made their own fermented concoctions from grain or corn. Later on, *Pulque* and *Mescal* were popular but these drinks had devastating effects on people. Its production was unsanitary while its sale was mostly in filthy squalid bars.

The thousands of people that made the annual pilgrimages to the god of drunkenness, Ome Tochtli in Tepoxtlaá, often arrived grubby and sodden, goofy from over consumption of cheap pulque. So when German immigrants and the influence of a brief 'Habsburg' rule over Mexico in the middle of the 19th century happened, modern-day beer brewing became an all-Mexican endeavor.

The Austrian Emperor Maximilian ruled Mexico for only four years, but had a lasting effect on the future of beer consumption in Mexico. This chap never traveled without his brew-masters. As a result, two brands of Mexican beer, Negra Modelo and Dos Equis Ámber, are like the darker, more malty subset of German lagers known as 'Vienna style'.

While not as heavy as most British ales, the Mexican 'Viennas' are fuller bodied with more malty sweetness and character than pale pilsners.

The first commercial lager beer brewery in Mexico was La Pila Seca, founded in 1845 by a Swiss immigrant. Soon there was the opening of the Cervecería Toluca y México, by another Swiss brewer and in 1869 Cerveceria Cruz Blanca was founded in Mexico City. While at first, most breweries were small operations, by 1890, the first substantial industrial brewing facility in Mexico was build in Monterrey for Cervecería Cuauhtémoc.

Prohibition in the United States boosted the Mexican brewing industry in the 1920ies as Americans flocked to border cities to purchase and went crazy on alcohol. Several new breweries opened on the Mexican side of the border in places such as Tecate and Mexicali.

Today, most Mexican beers are produced by the two beer giants, FEMSA and Grupo Modelo. FEMSA which is now owned by the Dutch brewery Heineken, has about 44% market share and is a general beverage corporation whose roots date back to 1890 and that first large Mexican brewery in Monterrey. With their brands; Tecate, Sol, Dos Equis, Carta Blanca, Superior, Indio, Bohemia and Noche Buena – FEMSA is a major international brewery. Grupo Modelo, the competition of FEMSA, has fewer brands but is actually larger with more than half of the market share due in part of its export. They make the famous Corona, Corona Light, Negra Modelo, Modelo Especial, Modelo Light, and Pacífico and Victoria.

The Mexican market is the world's eighth-largest by volume and Corona is the most popular Mexican brew outside of Mexico. The strange thing is however, that some Mexican brands are hard to come by in some parts of Mexico. Carta Blanca for one, while it is such a great beer. One beer critique describes it as *"The best Mexican beer I've ever had, and easily one of the best lagers overall. It compliments Mexican food so well, it's unbelievable. It has a nice flavor, high in alcohol, no hint of being watered down. This makes Corona look like tap water".*

Talking about water, did you know that for every liter of beer most breweries need about six to eight liters of water? For that, it is interesting to read a recent statement made by Anheuser-Busch, the world's number one beer maker headquartered in Brussels Belgium. In light of a 'Better World' commitment, it is trying to reduce water consumption during the brewing process. They targeted to use only 3.5 hecto-liters of water for each hecto-liter of beer by the end of 2012. That's a huge reduction, fine as long as the quality of the beer does not suffer because of it. One thing I noticed since Heineken has taken over FEMSA; my favorite Dos Equis Amber is now finally for sale in Baja.

Thanks Ome Tochtli.

-0-0-0-0-

National Margarita Day

February 22 is one of those completely made up and unnecessary holidays that you can't help but love because it makes for a valid excuse to throw a party. Who was the smart-ass that came up with the idea to call February 22 National Margarita Day is just as mysterious as who invented the margarita. The fact is that next to tequila and Corona, the margarita is the epitome of Mexican drinks that has become incredibly popular on both sides of the border. With National Margarita Day you are invited to try new recipes and get together with friends to toast on this delightful cocktail.

As for the origin of the margarita, it is like the many stories about who invented the pizza. Many places claim to have invented the margarita but nobody really knows. For that reason, the stories about the inception of the margarita cocktail are as numerous as the variations on its recipe. Some accounts are quite vague, others are far fetched. I am not chauvinistic, but the most likable story claims the origin to be right here in Baja California. The northern part of Baja that is, in a bar at the Riviera del Pacifico Hotel and Casino in Ensenada to be exact. In 1938 Danny Herrera, a renowned Mexican bartender at the casino was completely in love with Marjorie King, an American actress who hated taking tequila pure while tequila was also the only liquor that her body could tolerate. Finicky girl as she was, Herrera used his ingenuity to impress her and mixed the best ingredients to meet Marjorie's predicament. A third of tequila, a third Triple Sec and a third of fresh lime juice made Marjorie, who was called Margarita in

Mexico, utterly happy. The word spread around and soon enough the 'Margarita' became one of the world's most famous cocktails.

Another tale that traces the origin of the margarita back to Baja sounds more believable then the previous one. Enrique Bastate Gutierrez from Tijuana claims to have created the Margarita as homage to actress Rita Hayworth, whose real name was Margarita Cansino. As a teenager, Margarita Cansino worked as a dancer at the Foreign Club, in Tijuana, where she inspired the bartender's creativity which resulted in this famous cocktail. This was obviously before Hayworth adopted her screen name, which dates the origin of the margarita back to mid-1930. There are many more stories about the invention of the margarita and some of them can be found in 'The Great Margarita Book', a 146-page colorful and informative creation by Al Lucero with a foreword by Robert Redford. The latter is obviously an extreme margarita connoisseur while Lucero has been mixing and serving margaritas for over 20 years at the bar in the famous Maria's Restaurant in Santa Fe, New Mexico. The second edition has 90 recipes of tasty margaritas that are basically prepared the same way but with the emphasis on different ingredients. The descriptions in variation of tequilas from ordinary *reposado* to premium and super-premium can be a true eye opener.

National Margarita Day challenges us to try different recipes which can give you real insight about the subtle differences between tequila. A good margarita, crushed, on ice or straight up never tastes better than on a sunny patio around a pool or on the beach. For everyday happy hour I keep mine simple, but perhaps for this

special occasion I might try a premium tequila in my margarita. A simple recipe is as follows; two parts of reasonable tequila, one part of Controy and one part of fresh squeezed lime with some course sea-salt to balance it off. If you want to tone it down a notch or keep your weight under control, try a Margarita Light.

This concoction saves calories as well as your mental and physical abilities. Take 1 1/2 oz. tequila, 2 oz. diet lemon-lime soda, 3 oz. diet lemonade, a splash of lime juice on 1 cup of Ice. For a dazzling array of other Margarita recipes, there is a book '101 Margaritas by Kim Haasarud. Around 10 dollars at Amazon. This is an amazing compilation of margarita recipes with one for every colour coordinated occasion and events throughout the year.

-0-0-0-0-

If Mescal would be a guy, Tequila could be his sister

Not that tequila is for sissies, but mescal, which seems to gain huge popularity lately, is with its earthy and smoky taste definitely a guys drink while tequila is often enjoyed by both genders. Not long ago, in Mexico's back country it was often difficult to find tequila. Instead all they had was bootlegged hooch and the firm belief that it would raise a man's soul to its true height.

Mescal was the catchall term for these spirits distilled from different varieties of the agave plant and usually sold in recycled plastic soda bottles. Therefor mescal has always been looked upon as a cheap alternative to tequila. But that has changed as some producers have found methods to refine their product and set up ways to export their mescal to trendy bars and restaurants in the southern US and Canada.

Mescal is produced from the maguey plant (member of the Agave family) and was one of the most sacred plants in pre-Hispanic Mexico as it was used in religious rituals.

Unlike tequila, which comes from the blue agave and a restricted area, the maguey plant can be found all over Mexico but the production for mescal is mainly in the state of Oaxaca. According to Wikipedia there are 330,000 hectares cultivated for mescal and owned by about 9,000 producers. They make over six million liters annually with more than 150 brand names.

The origin of mescal is not certain, but there is a myth, as there are about so many things in Mexico. It is said that a lightning bolt struck an agave plant that instantly cooked the inside and opened it, releasing its juice. For this reason, the liquid is called the "elixir of the gods." Before the Spaniards invaded the new World, Aztecs were able to distill a drink called Pulque. Apparently, the Spaniards didn't like that too much and as their stock of European brandy ran out, (they learned distillation from the Moors some 700 years earlier) they started to experiment with local plants.

Now there is a long tradition of handcrafting mescal on a small-scale. A village in the state of Oaxaca can contain several production houses, called *palenques*, each using methods that have been passed down from generation to generation. Some of them are using the same techniques from 200 years ago. The process begins by harvesting the plants. This is a heavy job as the spiky leaves have to be sheared from the maguey, making them look like huge mutant pineapples. The heart or piña, can take the size of a laundry basket and can weigh 80 to 170 pounds each. Once they have enough, the *piñas* are cooked for about three days in underground pit ovens. This roasting in earthen mounds over pits of hot rocks gives mescal its intense and distinctive smoky flavor. Once that process is finished the *piñas* are crushed and mashed traditionally by a Flinstonian wheel, called a tahona which is pulled and turned by a mule or a donkey. The mash is then left to ferment in large vats or barrels with added water. At this point it only makes for a beverage with the strength of beer or wine which calls for distillation to make it stronger.

Just like with tequila, there is even a secondary distillation involved making it a strong 78-80 proof (38-40% alcohol) drink. Depending on the duration and the containers the end product is kept in, you get like with tequila, the general classifications such as plain *blanco*, *reposado* (two months old) or *añejo* (over a year on oak). There are a lot of varieties in mescal due to added spices, flavors added and differences in processes, like chicken can be added in the tank during distillation making for a typical taste besides the smokiness. Then there is 'gusano' or gusanito, the mescal with the famous worm in the bottle.

Mescal is seldom used in cocktails but consumed pure and preferably with Oaxaca cheese or *chapulines* (fried grasshoppers) on the side. There is a well know saying about drinking mescal: *"para todo mal, mescal, y para todo bien también"* translating into "for everything bad, there is mescal; for everything good there is the same." And as for its popularity outside of Mexico, the US and Japan buy most of the 25 million dollars worth of export. At Poblano Escobar, a popular bar in LA., they have moved away from the traditional pure mescal and developed a cocktail called Mayan sacrifice and 400 Rabbits. According to a patron, *"this cocktail has just enough balance of spiciness and smokiness to bring tears to your eyes"*. Other bars in LA. with an interesting mescal selection are Las Perlas and El Diablo. I was just in Vancouver Canada, where at La Mescaleria, an upstage bar/restaurant had a special on: 4 meat tacos, 1 Pacifico and a shot of tequila or mescal for $18. So this way, even far outside Mexico one can support the 29,000 people that are apparently working in the mescal production.

Salud!

-0-0-0-0-

What about Mexican wine?

There is actually a pretty extensive history of wine in Mexico. Not much has been documented and expectations have not been very high until recently. The first grapes, Vitis Vinifer, were brought to the Americas, North and South, from Europe and were planted in Mexico by the Spanish in the early 1500s. This was long before they arrived in any other part of the New World. After unsuccessful attempts by Spanish conquistadors to grow wine grapes in the tropical areas of Mexico, cuttings were planted alongside the native varietals which grew abundantly in Parras Valley in the State of Coahuila. Soon after grapes were introduced to other regions such as Puebla and Zacatecas. Nobody knows for sure what the initial grape varietal was that first crossed the Atlantic, but what we know is the grape was referred to as the common black grape of Spain, and that it gave rise to the mission grape of California, the Criolla Grande.

The planting of vinifera grapes was ordered by Hernan Cortes around 1520 after the supply he had brought dwindled. During the next century and a half wine production in Mexico skyrocketed.

Casa Madero, the first commercial winery, was established by Lorenze Garcia in Santa Maria de las Parras (Coahuila) in 1597 and is still in operation today, making it not only the oldest Mexican winery, but the oldest in the entire Americas.

Over time, the demand for Spanish wine imports dropped off which resulted in a ban in 1699 on wine production in the country save for church requirements. This ban was not officially lifted until Mexico's independence.

The ban of course, did not stop the Mexican wine producers entirely. Juan Ugarte, a Jesuit priest, was one of the many who continued making wine despite the ban.

He introduced the first vines to Baja California upon his relocation to Loreto in 1701. From there the vines were transported to Santo Tomas Mission south of Ensenada. Things moved slowly in those days, so it took the Jesuits to 1791 to establish the Santo Tomas Mission. And then it took another half century before they worked the exceptional fine soil conditions in the Guadalupe Valley, a short distance north of Ensenada. By that time, in 1843, it was the thirsty Dominicans who started wine production at the Mission Nuestra Senora de Guadalupe del Norte.

During the next 50 years, the era of wars had a pretty negative effect on wine making in Mexico. The vineyard's land was seized by the state and redistributed. However, in 1888 the Santo Tomas Mission was revived as a commercial winery by private investors and now operates as Bodegas Santo Tomas. From that period until 1910 wine-making spread once again. A group of Russian immigrants (the Molokans) fled the Czar's army in Europe and relocated to the Guadalupe Valley and surrounding areas. There they began making good quality wines, only to be stifled by the Mexican Revolution.

Much later, in the 1980s there has been a small revival again especially in the Guadalupe Valley. Foreign competition and a general lack of good grape varieties and agricultural knowledge made it still a struggle. Over time and with imported skills and experience from France and Italy, some small wineries have sprung up since the 90s. Now they have started to produce some excellent wines that can match any product from the Napa Valley.

In August every year, the Guadalupe Valley in Northern Baja hosts *Fiesta de la Vendimia,* a grandiose wine and food tasting event spread over several weeks while the grapes in the area are ripening for the next harvest. *Vendimia* means 'harvest of wine-grapes' which will be soon following the fiesta. At times there can be more then half a dozen events going on simultaneously on one day. From actual crushing of grapes and live music performances to Tango shows and candlelight dinners.

Talking about Mangoes
from a talk on the phone with my Mexican house-sitter

"Wow, your mango tree looks good this year," Agustin said.

"Yes," I said, "you must have many new mangoes."

"Yeah, that will be lots of mango juice for me," said Agustin (because I will not be there when they are ripe).

"Mangoes to peel and eat. Mango paste, mango pasta, you name it," Agustin rubbed in.

"You know," I said, "It will take two to mango, and I am not there."

"Oh, but I have lots of friends. A mango here, a mango there, mangos everywhere," he said.

"We'll eat succulent Mangoes until we die."

Mangoes are delicious in smoothies, luscious in salsa but can be a slimy, slippery challenge to cut. The best way to go about it is to start first with a ripe, but still firm fruit. If the mango is too ripe, it will be a mushy mess, and hard to cut into pieces, though easy enough to scoop out for pulp.

Late summer when they are ripe, the town has a Mango Fiesta. Food and music are hugely intertwined at most fiestas.

Now this is how you attack a mango. Look at the mango and realize it has a flattish oblong pit in the center of it. Your objective is to cut along the sides of the pit, separating the flesh from the pit. Holding the mango with one hand, stand it on its end, stem side down. Standing the mango up like this you should be able to imagine the alignment of the flat, oval pit inside. With a sharp knife in your other hand, cut from the top of the mango, down one side of the pit. Then repeat with the other side. You should end up with three pieces - two halves, and a middle section that includes the pit.

Next, take a mango half and use a knife to make length- and crosswise cuts in it, but try not to cut through the peel. At this point you may be able to peel the segments right from the peel with your fingers. Or, you can use a small paring knife to cut away the pieces from the peel.

Last, take the mango piece with the pit, lay it flat on the cutting board. Use a paring knife to cut out the pit and remove the peel.

-0-0-0-0-

National Nacho Day

There is this trend of celebrating special food days, like a pizza day, donuts day, or taco day. You name it, and there is a day claimed on the calendar for a certain food, either spontaneously invented by an influential foodie or by marketing from a particular company. So there is a particular food for every day of the year. October 4 2016 was National Taco Day and November 6 is ordained to 'National Nacho Day.' This of course, fits perfectly in the ex-pat's lifestyle as they try to have a good time anywhere in Mexico and have easy access to good nachos.

Now what is considered a good nacho, varies of course from person to person. Originally nachos were rather simple, small tortillas with cheese and salsa. Nowadays we throw a lot more stuff on there so they can replace a whole meal. Wikipedia describes nachos as a popular food based on nixtamalized corn, of Mexican origin that can be either made quickly to serve as a snack, or prepared with more ingredients to make a full meal. This nixtamalized word can be a bit of a tongue-crusher but is no joke and comes from nixtamalization. This is a process that entails the preparation of maize, corn or other grain, in which the product is soaked and cooked in an alkaline solution, usually lime-water, and then hulled or husked from its protective outer layer. In their simplest form, nachos are tortilla chips covered in melted or shredded cheese, salsa and sliced jalapeño.

Nachos originated in the city of Piedras Negras, Coahuila, around 1943, at a restaurant called the Victory Club. This town is just over the border from Eagle Pass, Texas, and home to a military base. What happened, and this is apparently a true story, the wives of several US soldiers from nearby Eagle Pass were in

49

Piedras Negras on a shopping trip and arrived at the restaurant after it had just closed for the day. The ladies must have begged chef Ignacio Anaya to make them something, so Ignacio, called 'Nacho,' threw a dish together for them with what little he had available in the kitchen: tortillas and cheese. He cut the tortillas into triangles and fried them, then added yellow Wisconsin cheese and called the dish Nachos Especiales, or Nacho's Specialty.

From there, the popularity of the "nacho" spread throughout Texas and the word "nachos" appeared in an English dictionary for the first time in 1949. It took however, another 20 years before the nacho became popular outside of Texas. In the 70's, the popular sports journalist Howard Cosell was given a plate of nachos during a taping of Monday Night Football, and liked them so much, he kept talking about them for weeks, which introduced the nacho to a whole new audience. Later on, Ignacio went on to work at 'The Moderno Restaurant', in Piedras Negras, and eventually opened up his own Nacho restaurant in the same town. And now until this day, both places still use the original recipe. You don't have to be in Mexico to find an interesting variation, from the simple or plain nacho to the piled up, like a mountain high plate of nachos with ingredients from here to Acapulco; this is something you can try anywhere or anytime. But on November 6, it is worth celebrating 'national nacho day' in a restaurant or at home. With the right company and enough *cervezas*, you can have a sweet party that will carry you over until bigger events will take place later in the month.

Around the House

Casita Azul

The casita sure was blue, cute, with an outside shower and a large open space with a palapa roof, hidden between huge bamboo and fruit trees. We moved in just in time to enjoy happy hour on the patio while the soft evening sun spread a beautiful light through the palm trees.

At night however, we got a different feeling about the place. Cold as it became, tiny geckos came alive and were running all over the adobe walls and ceilings, everywhere. My wife panicked.

"I am going to die! If one falls off the ceiling into my bed!" she yelled.

A moment later I saw a seven-centimeter-long (nearly 3"), black creature crawling on the kitchen counter. I was not sure if cockroaches came that large and was not going to look it up in a reference book, so I crushed the sucker with the bottom of a wine bottle real fast. It gave me the creeps, and suddenly we were not that happy couple on a Mexican vacation any more. All night I heard sounds like mice crawling in or along the palapa roof. Every five minutes I heard something fall down near the kitchen counter. I went up to investigate with a flashlight thinking, if this were more of those roaches, with the frequencies of 12 per hour, there would be sixty or seventy of them crawling around tomorrow morning. I could not shake the idea, what a disaster it would be to try to kill them all. However, wherever I looked, I could not find anything. I waited in the cold to hear the sound, but of course nothing happened when you look for it. I went back to bed and turned the flashlight off, but kept it really close.

Another night now, we had an enormous windstorm. No problems inside other than the noise, but the next morning we see thousands of little black pins, like small seeds, on the patio.

51

While having breakfast out there, one of those exceptional mornings here in Todos Santos this time, I see one of the seeds move. There was no wind.

Soon I saw a few more moving. I swear, I had no rum in my coffee. The little pins were changing from tiny round seeds to oblong, moving objects in a matter of minutes. I still had trouble defining what they really were, but my wife was not going to wait for that. She took the broom and got rid of it real fast. A few were left here and there and as it turned out, they walked away as little ants an hour or so later. So the wind on the patio must have blown all the larvae out of the palapa during the night. We could have come back a day later with thousands of ants over the house. How do people deal with this I wondered, if you leave a house unattended for some weeks or months. I guess you can be in for quite a surprise if you come back after six months.

-0-0-0-0-

Curious or what?

Not so horrifying as the previous story, but when we were renting a casita for a month right on the *Malecón*, I noticed something strange happening each night. Tonight, I finally came to write it down as I have been noticing the phenomenon for some time now, but could not believe it until I confirmed it.

Every evening around six O'clock a police car comes by and stops at our corner. A guy jumps out, opens, and closes an electrical box on the wall and leaves in a hurry. He goes so quickly and nothing happens, as it appears. What was he doing?

Tonight I went to the box to investigate. It just sits there open and is not protected, so I open it and see a switch and a lot of wires, some bare and exposed. I realized that it must be the light switch for the lights on the boulevard. Neon light, that takes some time as nothing happens for maybe ten minutes. Once they are heated up, they start to glow. That's why I could not link the police car and the boulevard lights. However, the scary part is, that the box with exposed wires is accessible to anyone. Even a kid could put their hands in it. Imagine what could happen? Should I have turned them off? Maybe it would have reduced the number of noisy visitors on the *Malecón* at night.

After years of traveling around Mexico, staying in hotels and renting places we decided to find our own place.
If you ever consider buying property in Mexico, the next part is of great importance to you.

Different Kind of Properties

Many people that have vacationed in the popular beach destinations know all about 'Time Shares.' The sales people can be very pushy and folks are often trapped into something they later regret. Also, a week or two is not going to cut it if you like to live or retire in Mexico.

So, Time Share is out.

One has to make first the distinction between Restricted Zone and Non Restricted land in Mexico as any land or property in the Restricted Zone has some complications for foreigners. A 50 kilometre strip along the entire Mexican coastline, East and West, is a restricted area for reasons to keep control over who owns what. Land border areas have even a wider strip, 100 km. that require special arrangements. Those old laws were revised in 1973 to accommodate foreign buyers. A Bank-Trust system called *Fideicomiso* was established which is a smart form of a 'milk-cow' set up by the Mexican government to keep a finger in the pot of all property owned by foreigners in border areas. This trust is held by a Mexican bank which will hold the property for a maximum duration of 50 years. The ocean is being considered a border also, requiring all property in Baja to have a bank trust which costs about 500 USD per year to keep up. The good news is that most Mexican banks are as good and trustworthy as most US banks are nowadays. There is no difference in use of the property for foreign owners and the trust is also fully transferable. It is just a lot of extra paperwork and expense to set it up and the yearly retaining fee to maintain.

Purchasing real-estate in Mexico is a very complex transaction with many pitfalls. In my next book, 'Living or Retiring in Mexico', there is a large chapter on buying property and how to avoid disappointment with serious transactions.

Ever cut off from electricity?

Regular electricity is for one who has lived on solar for five years very nice and pretty easy to get used to. We always got by on our solar panels that were hooked up to eight deep-cycle batteries. I had to be careful when my wife was ironing and I used the sander or the drill at the same time. Same thing if we had three or four days of overcast in a row, but when does that happen in southern Baja?

One day we had a real problem. A few days before Christmas one year, when after some not so sunny days, I forgot to turn off the huge strings of outdoor Christmas lights at our driveway. We were not completely out of juice, but the system did shut off to protect the batteries from discharging below 20 percent. This is the amount set on most inverters to avoid damage to the batteries. That doesn't mean that there is no power left, but it made my wife rather panicky when the coffee maker didn't turn on that morning. I turned everything off in the house and we waited for the sun to come out, which brought our power back again.

The incident however made us aware of how vulnerable we were and once CFE (the National electricity provider) came into our neighborhood with 24/7 juice on a wire, we decided to hook up. The application is not complicated. You fill out a small questionnaire and you have to have proof of domicile, like a water bill in your name will suffice. The actual connection is more problematic if it is going to be a first time. You are responsible for setting up the meter in a small cement structure at the edge of your property. If you don't go under ground, the piping has to go upwards to a certain height so the wires can be connected from across the street if needed without hanging too low for traffic

. Also, you are responsible for the connection from the meter-box down and to the house. In my case to the bodega, where I have the main panel, batteries and inverter, out of the way of the elements.

For the months we are back up north we have a house sitter. Last summer he also went away for some time and the electric bill that comes normally every other month, got lost somehow in the process. He insists he never saw a bill. It's possible that it blew away during one of those nasty summer storms. Anyway, the account did not get paid and CFE doesn't give you much slack. They cut you off pretty quick and by the time we came back in November, we were still on solar power only. That was not in our plan, so I went to the CFE office in town with the last paid bill to get reconnected again. To bring that bill was smart. It made it very easy to look up the account and all I had to do was to pay 450 pesos re-connection fee and the outstanding balance. The big question now was when the power would be back on again. I asked the girl at the office and she tells me "mañana."

"Yeah right," I said. "Everything here is mañana. Seriously?" She said again "mañana." Oh well, I thought, we will find out and I left the office with rather low expectations. The next day we had to go to La Paz and when we came back that afternoon, I could not wait to find out. A small *milagro* had happened. Our power was back on. Who would expect such efficiency in Mexico? However, for next summer, I hope to avoid the whole fuss by pre-paying the account. Apparently you can do that with CFE and also with your water bills. The amounts are not huge, and it will make life a lot simpler for us gringos. Cheers to CFE for outstanding service.

-0-0-0-0-

For Shade, Palm Trees come in handy

In a sunny country, shade is important. So this is 101 on palm trees. Ever heard of a Jelly Palm? The other day I was browsing at a nursery for some high scrubs as I needed to create some shade and privacy between my place and the neighbors. As it was basically to protect me from the view they have from their second floor guest casita, located above their garage, the tree I was looking for should be at about 12'-18' tall.

At that height, palms come to mind, but it can take a long time before they will grow to that level. Even ordinary Washingtonians, the poor-man's palm, can take 5 or 6 years before they reach my required height. And the problem then is that they keep growing, as they can reach 80-90 feet and become bare at 18 or 20 feet level. So I went looking for other species and got myself informed on the much prettier Royal palm. Scientific name is Roystonea and Wikipedia tells me that the 'royal' is just one of eleven species of monoecius palms, native to the Caribbean Islands, and the adjacent coasts of Florida and Central and South America.

An interesting fact is that this genus was named for Roy Stone, a US army engineer. But as the royal palm can reach heights of 130 ft, this one is not going to do the trick for me either. Most species in this group will grow between the 49'-66' range. It will take longer for what is left of my life-time to see the appropriate height.

Of course, there is a solution for that: transplant some more mature palms, but that becomes quite oppressive for my peso account.

You do see it more and more: whole palms including a massive clod of soil and roots transported through town. I went to see someone at a Vivero, as they call a nursery here, to find out what they recommend. The guy told me: Jelly' palms. What? Are you kidding? I have heard of jelly beans but never of jelly palms. So he told me that Butia Capitata, the official name for a Jelly Palm, is one of the hardiest feather palms, tolerating temperatures below freezing and is commonly grown on the East Coast of the United States as far north as Virginia Beach, Virginia and West up to Seattle, Washington. We joked about climate change and how I wished we didn't need such a hardy palm here in Baja.

I explained my need to obscure the neighbors casita at a certain height. And then he was right on the ball when he told me that this palm grew up to 18-20 ft., exactly what I needed. He showed me some mature Jelly palms as we walked over the grounds to the back of his vivero.

At home I looked up some more on the Jelly palm and found out that it carried edible fruit. Ripe Jelly palm fruit is about the size of large cherries, and yellowish/orange in color. The taste is a mixture of pineapple, apricot, and vanilla according to Wikipedia.

The taste can vary depending on soil conditions, perhaps some banana taste can be detected. It is tart and sweet at the same time, with flesh similar to a loquat (Chinese plum), but slightly more fibrous.

The last fact is an absolute bonus if you realize that the pulp is a good source of Beta Carotene and pro-vitamin A according to Juliana Pereira Faria, PhD who published her findings in an abstract.

Years ago, the mansion at the end of our road got four truckloads, those long 16-wheeler, with mature palms delivered and planted and then they found out they were not the Royals but the rather poor looking Mexican Washingtonians. Not good enough of course for a mansion, so a few weeks later they were pulled out and new truckloads arrived late at night to put the right ones in. Money was obviously no object. I am in a different category, but the more I found out about the Jelly palm, the stronger I was motivated to order a few mature ones and just hope they will catch on as I will invest most of my peso account to regain my privacy, and more importantly; shade, and perhaps have some healthy fruit along the way.

-0-0-0-0-

The 'Mordida

This is the common term for 'bribe,' which feels apparently like 'a bite' as the word really means in Spanish. Another term in our language is 'kick-back' and it is not always clear who gets kicked or bitten. I am sure you have heard horror stories about the Federal police bribing folks using the road in Mexico. Over the 12 years we have been driving in Mexico, and often for five or six months a year, we got bribed only three times.

When it happens, it actually comes as a shock to you, so it is absolutely not fun. You should not go along with it, if you can avoid it. Meaning, play dumb or use another language then Spanish or English to confuse them unless there is ground for holding you up because you made a clear traffic violation.

Once we got away with that, but the first time it happened, it did not. It was early morning, little traffic in Tijuana and we had bikes on top of the car, too easy to spot. This guy on a motorbike flagged us down, and I doubted that he even was a real policeman. I asked ID and he showed me something that did not convince me entirely. He asked for 100 dollars. I asked him for what?

"You were speeding over 80 in a 50 zone."

I was certain that I had not and we argued back and forth for some time. He was not letting go, and insisted to get us to the Tijuana police station. Well that must scare even the most hardened people, because that is the last place you ever want to end up.

So that worked for him, but as we just arrived over the border, we had no pesos in the equivalent amount and while driving through the states we basically use plastic, so we had no dollars either.

We told him that we had some Canadian money and reluctantly, he would accept that. We got my wife's wallet and cleaned it out entirely for which he provided a used brown envelope. He was looking around him before he dropped the envelope through my side window and all we could find was 32 Canadian and some change. I put it in the dirty envelope and handed it back to him. Without looking in to it, he took off and so did we, rather shocked from this early morning encounter.

The other two times were in La Paz, southern Baja. Again, minimal infractions, both ignoring a stop sign, which most locals do but your foreign license-plate is quickly noticed and taken advantage of. It also depends on what time of year. This was close to Christmas with an obviously strong need for cash to buy the kids presents.

Again, it felt bad, and it made one reason to decide importing our little car and put Mexican plates on it so we are not such an easy target any more.

-0-0-0-0-

Acknowledgements

First I'd like to thank my wife of nearly 50 years, Marianne who traveled with me and with whom I shared these many experiences, most pleasant some not so pleasant, while living in Mexico. She played an integral role in our lives in Mexico and encouraged me to write this book and made my sometimes steep learning curve, manageable.

To my friends and family, let me express my gratitude in helping me to decide on the right cover. And last but not least, the content was tirelessly proofread and edited by Wendy Tippett, Tony Hargreaves and Stuart Swain. Without you, this book wouldn't be readable.

As this book has a selection and excerpts from bigger things to come, I hope to receive the same support for the full-size book. 'Living or Retiring in Mexico' will soon come out in print.
Both products are my own creation and I apologize for any imperfections, changed conditions or facts as Mexico is a very dynamic country where change can happen rather rapidly.

-0-0-0-0-

Did you like what you read?

To help other people find this book, there are several ways to accomplish that.
Word of mouth recommendations are probably the oldest form and still work.
Social media is not exactly the same, but talking about 'Taste of Mexico' might help others to find it. And finally, posting an online review at your favorite book site would be much appreciated and would also spread the word about 'Living in Mexico'

Check out the next book on Mexico;

'Living or Retiring in Mexico?'
-This is what you need to know-

Available soon on-line or at your bookstore
ISBN 978-0973552751

Or send me your e-mail (leoBuijs@yahoo.ca) to order your special autographed copy

Made in the USA
Charleston, SC
29 October 2016